In the Summertime

M.J. Sherman

ISBN 978-1-64007-923-6 Paperback

ISBN 978-1-64007-922-9 Hardcover

Published by: Book Services
                www.BookServices.us

Contents

🔲 = Illustrations

Dedication

To my mom and dad, my grandparents, and my aunts and uncles, who gave me a childhood made magical by summers at the little red cottage on Lake Winnebago. Thank you for giving me the freedom to go anywhere my imagination would take me, the freedom to explore, to invent crazy pastimes with my siblings and cousins, and to enjoy hours of solitude when I needed it.

M.J. Sherman

Chapter 1
The Red Cottage

The red cottage sat silent and empty, anticipating our return. The sun glistened on the water. A fish jumped, water droplets cascading from its fins, and the sudden splash broke the silence. The ripples spread slowly across the surface of the lake and lapped quietly against the dock. A flock of gulls screamed as they dove at the fish. A soft breeze kissed the water near shore and carried the scent of the lake to us as we neared it.

We had arrived for our summer at the lake.

Grandpa B built our first cottage in stages from the late 1930s to the early 1940s. It was on Lake Winnebago 15 miles from town. But our first cottage met its sad demise before I was born.

Shortly after my father graduated from high school, the family was spending the weekend at the cottage. Dad was out sailing with some friends. Grandpa and Grandma and Aunt Emmy Lou were relaxing outside, watching the comings and goings on the lake and enjoying the peace and quiet of a warm summer day.

Grandpa suddenly became aware of dark clouds piling up across the lake.

The coming of a storm at the lake meant everyone had to hustle. Lawn chairs must be put up against the cottage; the hammock needed to be taken in; and anything loose had to be tied down or sheltered near the cottage.

A storm over the lake almost always boded *sturm und drang*: thunder, lightning, high winds, and even a rare tornado, like the one that hit the north end of the lake in 1965. Grandma asked Grandpa if he thought that Dad would be okay. After all, a bunch of young boys having fun on the lake might not be paying attention to the weather. Grandpa just said, "He's smart enough to pay attention. He'll come in before it gets bad."

So the three of them sat indoors to wait it out. They had done it before; they could do it again.

All at once Grandpa's attention was drawn to something moving on the floor. He put his newspaper aside and stared, awestruck. Dancing around on the floor were little globes of ball lightning. He watched them for a moment, stood up, and told Grandma and my aunt to gather up their things and get into the car.

They drove back to town through the rain and thought nothing more about the storm. Later in the week Grandpa was at the hardware store. Earl, the owner, walked over to him and asked if he had been at the lake since the storm. That must have worried Grandpa, for he went home, picked up Grandma and drove to the lake.

The cottage was gone. The only thing left was the chimney and a small glob of gold. Dad had left his watch on the mantel before he went sailing, and it had melted when the cottage burned.

Grandpa B rebuilt the cottage and painted it red. I don't know if that was as a reminder of the fire, or if it was just the cheapest paint Grandpa could find.

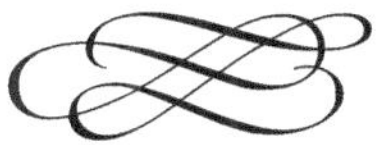

In the Summertime

Chapter 2
Cousins, Cousins, Everywhere

From the time I was two weeks old until I got married at nineteen, I spent my summers at our family cottage on Lake Winnebago, at 30 miles long and 10 miles wide, the largest lake in Wisconsin. As I look back on those interesting and idyllic summers, I realize how fortunate I was.

We had a close-knit community on "our" beach. Two cottages were occupied by my extended family and the rest were occupied by close friends. We didn't start out as friends, and several of the cottages changed hands over the years, but we were lucky enough to be surrounded by mostly wonderful, pleasant, interesting people.

I grew up thinking that it was too bad that everyone wasn't lucky enough to have a cottage and a wonderful group of people around them like we were. I wondered what those poor kids in New Holstein did all summer long. They couldn't possibly be as happy as I was.

We moved out to the cottage as soon as school was out in June. Except for occasional trips back to town to do laundry and shopping and to go to church on Sundays, we lived at the lake. Dad got up every morning, had breakfast with the family, and then drove into town to his job, returning by suppertime.

Most summers our cousins came from California. My aunt and cousins stayed for a month or two, but my uncle went back to California after his vacation time was up. That meant that most of the time, during the day, it was my mother, my aunt, Emmy Lou, and the seven of us cousins at the cottage. Emmy Lou felt like she was coming home because she was Dad's sister, and they grew up in New Holstein. My grandfather's brother owned the cottage next door, and his children and, eventually, his grandchildren, spent summers on the lake, too. I was a member of a family that came with ready-made summer playmates.

As young children we were allowed to run free, as long as we adhered to three rules. Everyone looked out for all of the kids on the beach without being "in their faces," because we learned those rules, both spoken and tacitly understood, at an early age.

Rule #1 — the rule you *never* broke — you could *not* go swimming unless you found an adult who agreed to watch while you were in the water.

Rule #2 — You must never, ever run on the pier. You could slip, loose your balance, or just not slow down in time.

These two rules prevented us from drowning. No child was ever lost to a serious accident. If an activity had anything whatsoever to do with the lake itself, an adult had to give their approval and either watch us or find someone who could.

Rule #3: If we wanted to go anywhere beyond the seven cottages that we considered our beach, we needed permission.

There were other, more flexible, rules that were not as vitally important, but those first three could not be broken or ignored. There were severe consequences for disobeying them.

The seven of us usually woke up early, put on our swimming suits, ate breakfast, and waited until a parent was willing to watch us. Then it was into the lake until we were either blue with cold or exhausted. We'd come out of the water, spread our towels in the sun, and eat the snack that Mom or Emmy Lou brought us. We often slept or dozed for a short period. Then it was back into the water until lunchtime. Before lunch we changed out of our suits and hung them, along with our towels, on the line to dry.

Chapter 3
The Shack

The shack was a shed-like building connected to the main cottage by a large screened-in porch. It provided sleeping accommodations for the young 'uns. There were six bunk beds, army-issue, made of 2 x 4s. They were a dull army green when Dad got them, but before they were installed in the shack, he painted them a bright and glossy sun yellow. A couple of bunks are still in the shack and they are still the same sunny color. For a number of years, there was a cot for the seventh child. That was me.

After lunch, we were required to rest for an hour. The younger cousins usually slept. The older ones could read but were not allowed to talk.

When naptime was over, we could put on our swimsuits again if we wanted to. Those who didn't were usually the ones who hadn't hung theirs up to dry. It's no fun struggling into a cold, wet, and clammy suit. In fact, it's one of the most unpleasant things I've ever done. We learned early on — or most of us did — to hang our suits on the line behind the shack if we wanted to swim later in the day.

As we grew older, we began to dislike naptime and couldn't understand why it continued to be a requirement. But after we became adults with families of our own, we all realized that naptime wasn't for us. It was for Mom and Emmy Lou. They needed a break from the seven of us, as well as from the assorted and sundry neighborhood children.

When we got older, naptime was suspended, but we were still required to stay out of the water for a time after lunch. I do believe that parents invented the myth of getting cramps if you didn't wait for an hour after eating was based on their need for postprandial peace and quiet. If they had a valid reason, we wouldn't be able to argue with them!

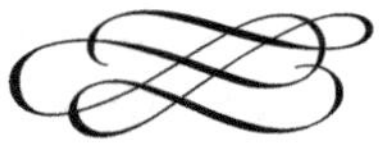

In the Summertime

Chapter 4
Bedtime Stories

Help! I'm Stuck!

When my cousin, John, and I finally got the oppor-
tunity to sleep in a bunk, we were still fairly young,
so Mom and Emmy Lou put six-inch-high boards
between the mattress and the front of the bunk. This
kept everybody safe and the blankets tucked tightly
around the mattresses. Yet somehow John managed
to fall off and break his arm. I, on the other hand,
had the opposite happen. John got untucked, but I got
overtucked.

Mom came out to the shack and tucked us in. She
said good night, kissed me on the cheek, and went
back into the cottage. Some time later, I woke up from
a sound sleep and couldn't move! I was pinned down!
I managed a muffled yell to my older sister. "Go get
Mommy, I'm stuck! And tell her to bring a knife!"

Bunk Bed in the Shack

Kris ran into the cottage, shouting, "Martha's stuck! Hurry! And bring a knife!"

Mom calmed Kris down and asked her to explain what was wrong. She did. Mom headed for the shack, Kris running along behind, repeating over and over, "You forgot the knife! She said to bring a knife."

Mom entered the shack, approached my bunk, and said softly, "Martha, turn around. Your head is at the bottom of the bunk, and your feet are on your pillow."

I did just that. I've had claustrophobia ever since, but I never fell off of my bunk.

Wake Up!

I had an odd experience years later. I had gone to bed and decided to read for a while. I must have fallen asleep while reading, because I was only vaguely aware of someone was talking to me.

My sister's friend, Juanita, was home for a visit and had decided to come out to the lake to visit Kris. When she got to the cottage, she noticed that it was mostly dark. Nita was a very good friend of the family, so she was comfortable coming out at that time of the night, and she also knew that someone would probably still be up reading.

Nita saw my light on, so she came into the room and sat down on the edge of the bed. We talked for about an hour. She asked me to tell Kris that she was only in town for a few days and would like to see her before she left again. I said I would be sure to tell Kris, and Nita left.

About a week later, Kris came storming into my room and, very loudly, asked me why I hadn't told her that Nita had stopped at the cottage when she was home. I asked her why she was yelling at me and why she thought I should tell her something that I couldn't possibly know.

She said that Nita had called to ask why she hadn't come to see her. Kris said she had no idea that Nita had been home. Nita then explained that she had come out to the cottage, seen a light on, and called softly. She explained that I had said, "Come on in," and we had talked for almost an hour, after which she had asked me to tell Kris she was home and I had assured her that I would.

The only conclusion we could come to was that I had actually visited with Nita, that I had been asleep when she came, and apparently hadn't been completely awake when we talked. That was the only time I've ever carried on a conversation while not totally awake. I wasn't sleep-walking, but I certainly was sleep-talking.

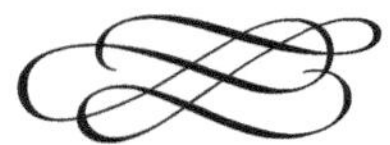

Chapter 5
Easter

Sometimes we went to the lake out of season. When I was two or three, the family went out to the cottage one Easter weekend. After that we often repeated our off-season visits. Sometimes there was ice on the lake; sometimes the water was open. But it was always chilly! And going there on Easter was especially exciting.

Before that first Easter visit, I worried. How did the Easter Bunny know that we would be at the lake? What if he hid all the Easter eggs out at the cottage, and then we stayed in town for Easter? We wouldn't have any eggs to find!

That particular Easter, Mom assured us that the Easter Bunny would know that we were going to the lake and he would hide our eggs there.

When we arrived at the cottage, we found that not only was the lake no longer frozen, but Uncle A.C.'s pier was already up. That was very unusual because we generally put our piers up on Memorial Day weekend.

Grandma B. offered to take the four of us out to look at the lake while Mom got the cottage warmed up and "found" the Easter baskets.

We walked over to A.C.'s pier next door. Grandma took Kris and me by the hand and sent Paul and Beth ahead of her. At some point, for reasons unknown, Grandma let go of my hand for a moment. When I saw her reach for my hand, I took two steps backwards. The second step took me into thin air and then into the lake. Grandma stood frozen for one horrified moment, then said just one word: "Beth!"

Beth turned around, saw me in the lake, and hesitating not a second, jumped in, clothes and all.

We were wearing our Easter finery, so it was imperative that we get out of the frigid water immediately! And believe me, the lakes of the Upper Midwest are excruciatingly frigid in early spring. Beth lifted me up. Grandma took me by both hands and set me back on the pier., then took my hand and Kris's hand and said, "Come!"

We all trooped back to the cottage. I did get to hunt for eggs, just not in my Easter finery.

For the next couple of years we did not go to the cottage for our Easter egg hunt. Even though she was older than I was, Kris was very worried too. "What if the Easter bunny hides our eggs out there, and we don't go to the lake? If he leaves them out there, we won't have any here to hunt for!"

Mom assured her that the Easter Bunny always knew where to hide the eggs. They would always be in the proper place, so Kris needn't worry.

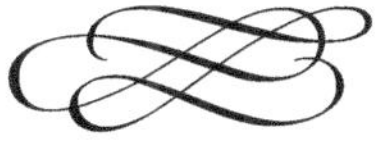

Chapter 6
Uncle A.C.'s Antics

Mealtime was just for families unless arrangements had been made beforehand. There was only one exception to that rule, self-made by Uncle A.C., Invariably, he would show up unannounced, outside our picture window. He would do something silly, or he'd be wearing some bizarre item of clothing.

I remember one time in particular. We had just started eating supper. Suddenly, Uncle A.C. popped up at the window, wearing a hat. Sticking out either side of his head was an arrow. He had a goofy look on his face, and he was dancing around like a nut. Mom got up and started toward the door. A.C. whipped off his hat, pulled on the wire that went over his head to hold the arrows in place, and hung his head like a naughty little boy.

By this time we were all laughing hysterically. When Mom finally reached the door, she was also laughing. All she could do when she opened the door was just try to wave him away. He swung his hat back onto his head, made a deep bow, and strode away. This sort of thing happened a lot more frequently than you would think and provided a great deal of amusement to the children.

Another of A.C.'s antics involved "the bell." A large brass bell hung on an iron post just above the beach on the lot line between our cottage and A.C.'s. It was installed when the first cottages were built in the mid-1930s and used to warn any fishermen out on the lake of approaching storms. No one was allowed to ring the bell for any reason other than its intended purpose.

Earl Schnell, one of our neighbors, A.C., and my grandfather had a tradition of pranking each other — and everyone else on the beach! Earl always rang the bell when he walked down the beach. A.C. always went out and scolded Earl.

One day, A.C. decided to teach Earl a lesson. He walked out to the bell, and keeping the clapper silent, carefully pulled on the rope, so that the bell tilted upside down, with the open end facing up. Then Uncle A.C. filled it with water and waited for Earl to show up.

About the time that Earl usually came by, Grandpa B., A.C.'s brother, went out to see why A.C. was standing stock still, looking up at the bell. They both stood looking at it in silence for a moment. Thinking the bell must be stuck, Grandpa finally said, "Oh for heav-

Uncle A.C.

en's sake. Just pull the cord." And he did, before A.C. could stop him. Well, Grandpa got doused with water just as Earl ambled by. He and A.C. had a good laugh, and after a while, Grandpa did too. For all of the years that A.C. lived at the lake, we all waited in breathless anticipation to see who would be the next victim, and what the next prank would be. Grandpa, A.C., and Earl never ran out of ideas.

Chapter 7
Hiking to Smiley's

There was a tiny village about a mile up the road from the lake. A poke and plumb town: by the time you could poke your head out of the car window, you were plumb out of town.

Often in the afternoon, when we were tired of swimming and were getting restless, we would gather up our nickels and dimes, and sometimes even pennies, and trudge the mile and a half up the hill to Smiley Nelson's store. There could be from two to ten of us. The store was small and old and crammed full of every imaginable thing in the world, or so it seemed to us. Many of the items in the store had been there far too long. There were faded sweatshirts, moldy oranges, rusty tools, and stale crackers. Few people actually shopped there, although occasionally someone would come in for an item desperately needed.

Smiley had the best penny-candy assortment in the universe. We'd all come traipsing into the store. Smiley would look up, give a slight nod of greeting, and go on about his business. We would make a tour of the store to see if anything had changed since the last time we were there. Then we'd make a u-turn and head for the rack of comic books. We'd perch on the edge of the windowsill or sprawl out on the floor around the rack. We were allowed to sit there and read as long as we were quiet and didn't get in the way of any other customers. When we grew tired of the comic books, we'd head for the candy counter.

Those of us who were too young to know how much candy we could get with our money would show Smiley what we had. We would start picking out our candy, and he would tell us when we had reached our limit. All of our candy would go into a small white paper bag. I know that there were many times when we got more than the amount that our pennies, nickels and dimes would buy.

One time, I walked up to the counter and plunked down my coins just as a lady stepped up. Mr. Nelson smiled at her and said, "I'll be with you in a minute, ma'am. I have to help this young lady first." While I picked out red licorice strips, black-licorice Scottie dogs, mints, chocolates, and lots of other goodies, Smiley quietly checked out the lady. Then he turned back to me. I'm sure that by that time, I had more than my quarter's worth.

Years later, when I was all grown up, I drove past the lot where Smiley's once stood. The store was gone. It had burned to the ground. My heart ached for a lost piece of my childhood.

In the Summertime

Chapter 8
Boom!

The Fourth of July was especially fun at the lake, because we always had a tremendous assortment of fireworks for our Independence Day celebration. This, despite the fact that the sale of commercial fireworks to private citizens in Wisconsin was illegal.

Jim, our neighbor down the road, was a farmer. That meant that he could buy fireworks for a legitimate purpose: to scare away blackbirds and crows that might otherwise destroy his crops.

Jim always arrived at the beach on the weekend of the 4th with at least two bushel baskets full of every kind of fireworks imaginable, many of which were designed to go boom. He'd have firecrackers and cherry bombs, Roman candles and bottle rockets, all very effective in scaring away the avian crowds. And there were sparklers.

We were allowed to choose what we wanted, but we were expected to be safe and responsible. It was all wonderfully fun, but we did have one minor accident when my cousin, Chrissie, burned a hole in her sweatshirt one year.

Sparklers were a favorite with all of us. Every year we were reminded not to drop the sparkler wires on the ground as someone might step on one and get hurt. We were also warned that if we dropped a wire on dry grass, we could start a fire.

Our parents set a bucket of water by the corner of our front patio. We were to extinguish the hot wires in the water. Chrissie was several cottages away when her sparkler went out. Since she couldn't put it down, and she wasn't near the bucket of water, she stuck it in her front sweatshirt pocket. One of the Laughton boys pointed to her and said, "Look! Chrissie is on fire tonight!"

It all ended well. The sparkler wasn't hot enough to burst into flame but it did burn a hole in her pocket.

The next year, and every year after that, several buckets of water were distributed along the beach. One minor accident: not a bad safety record for a dozen or more young people over years and years of Fourth of July celebrations.

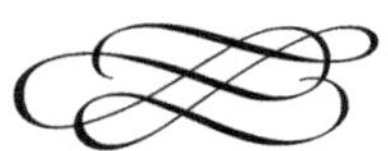

Chapter 9
The Fort

At one end of our neighborhood lake frontage, there was a wild swath of beach. The surface was mostly small pebbles on a bed of sand. An ancient cottonwood tree embraced almost the entire area. It had a huge, rough trunk with thick, gnarly limbs that reached out to frame a dark, mysterious chamber in which we built a small fort of found wood. Someone later erected a small, wooden shed that we used as clubhouse.

We discovered a myriad of unusual and fascinating treasures that had been washed ashore under the branches of that tree. There were clamshells with beautiful iridescent centers. There were stones of every imaginable shape, size, and color. There were pieces of sea glass that had been tumbled around by the waves until the edges were rounded and the surface roughened to a soft luminosity. The sea glass came in an infinite array of shapes and colors. The supply of driftwood was endless, some of it large enough for several of us to sit on, some of it so small we could fill our pockets with it every day and still not make a dent in the quantity strewn across the sand. This is just the short list of the precious objects that fired our imaginations.

We got to this place of wonder, "the point," by cutting across the front yard of what was to become my aunt's cottage. We walked across the lawn, stepped over big rocks, and ducked under the branches of the tree. We came out into a small chamber that we dubbed "the fort."

We girls played our games in the fort. When the others arrived, there was a war to see who could either hold or take the fort. In the end, we often wound up joining forces against an imaginary enemy, but sometimes the war ended with one side going way mad and plotting revenge.

It was a magical place for a young child. With only the found items and our imaginations, the fort could be any place and anything in the world.

I'm sure that the experience of growing up at the lake played a major role in my becoming the person I am today. The lake became so much a part of me, that for many years after I grew up and moved away from my hometown, the lake pulled at my heart so strongly that my husband would drive me (and later our children, too) to the lake for a sojourn of several weeks each summer. The need to go to the cottage was so powerful that I could never have said, "It's okay. We don't have to go." That would have been like saying, "I don't need to eat anymore to stay alive."

The yearning didn't ease until I was in my forties, and we bought a ranch in Oklahoma. Something about the shushing of the wind and the openness that surrounded us reminded me of the wide expanse of the lake. It wasn't exactly the same, but close enough to soften my longing for the red cottage and the lake.

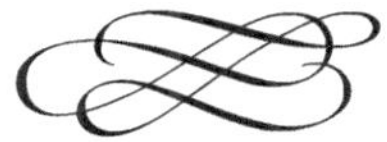

Chapter 10
Splash!

We all grew up being proficient in the water. No one ever had formal swimming lessons, but we could all handle ourselves in an emergency. Everyone of us, at one time or another, fell into the lake and had to be pulled out by one of the older kids or a nearby adult. Sometimes someone fell off one of the piers because they weren't paying attention. Sometimes someone fell in because they were roughhousing or because they just weren't very coordinated. And occasionally, you annoyed someone and they got revenge by throwing or pushing you into the lake — more on that later.

I fell in many times usually because I was trying to keep up with older siblings and cousins.

Once, when I was quite small, I was playing in the lake next to the pier. I had a small inner tube around my middle. I wasn't very lake-savvy yet, so I had to wear the inner tube to keep me upright. At least that was the idea. My eldest sister, Beth, was sitting on the pier "watching" me — with a book in her hands. (She later became a college professor.)

At one point she glanced up from her reading, and all she saw the inner tube and two feet kicking in the air. I was close enough to the dock that she dropped her book, leaned down, grabbed my feet. and lifted me out of the water. We never figured out how I got turned upside down with that thing around my middle, but no one ever read while watching kids in the water after that.

Now back to the subject of revenge. My brother, Paul, and his friend, Tom, were always pestering the rest of us. One day Beth and our cousin Paula decided to get back at Paul. They rounded up the rest of us, swore us to secrecy, and told us their plan: They'd get Paul out on the pier with some made-up reason, and we'd all push him into the lake.

Everything went according to plan until the last minute. At the last second, Paula changed her mind and switched sides. She pushed her sister, Susan, and Beth off the pier instead. Paula thought she had pulled off a great prank. We all had a different idea; she was obviously a traitor and would have to pay for her treachery.

Most of the cottages had fish tanks near the shore that were kept filled with water. The water came from artesian wells and it was icy cold.

Later that day, when Paula wasn't expecting it, Beth and Paul grabbed her and shouted at the four of us to open the fish tank. They got her over to the tank, and the rest of us grabbed her flailing arms and legs and stuffed her into the frigid tank. When it was over, Beth asked Paul why he'd helped us. He said, "You don't go back on an oath. The plan was to push me in and she didn't stick to it. So she got it back!"

As much time as we spent trying to" get" each other, when it came to getting together and carrying out some idea or plan, once you committed to it, you were expected to stick with it. Paula learned her lesson that day.

In the Summertime

Chapter 11
Rainy-day Amusements

Except for a few rainy-day items, we couldn't bring all our toys to the lake. Although we were allowed just one toy each., we never felt deprived. There was always something to see or do or some great discovery to make.

We may not have been allowed to bring our material possessions with us for the summer, but one thing we always had in abundance — our fertile imaginations. We had no problem finding endless ways to entertain ourselves.

It was just us and our make-believe worlds. We could be and do anything we wanted to. That was one of the major reasons that all of us loved being out at the lake.

Even on rainy days, there was a wealth of things to keep us occupied. We had lots and lots of books.

We had jigsaw puzzles and playing cards and board games. We had paper and pencils, crayons and paints. We played long, loud, fierce games of war and double solitaire and spent hours making up new card games.

Because we lived so close to the lake, we spent our entire summer at the cottage. The other families lived from one to three hours or more away, so they mostly spent just their weekends at the cottages. Occasionally, they would come for a week or two at a time. So on rainy days we (just the six or seven of us) spent the day on our screened porch. We had a picnic table and chairs out there. The older relatives and friends generally spent rainy days doing things like reading. We were seldom bored, even though we had no televisions or telephones. We had radios and record players. That was enough.

Did we feel isolated? We did not! There was just too much to do.

When a weekday was warm and sunny, I would lie in the hammock with a book if I could get there before my sisters, reading and dozing, but the rainy days didn't ruin our summers. They just gave us a different perspective.

Strange Ladies

The three sets of bunk beds in the shack where we slept were no ordinary bunk beds that could be found in a furniture store. They were heavy wooden bunks that had been painted bright yellow. They had been army bunks, and there were great big letters carved into the front board.

The letters were *U.S.* These had been army-issue bunks that either Dad or Grandpa B. had found at an army surplus store. We loved to imagine who might have slept in them.

My other Grandpa, my mother's father, built drawers to fit under the beds, two drawers for each bunk. They were supposed to be used for our clothes, but the drawers seemed to have a magnetic attraction for all sorts of other things — an accumulation of shoes, shells, rocks, and a variety of swimming towels of all sizes, shapes and designs.

The towels became the focus of our attention. When we were quite young we used the towels for dress-up. We turned them into everything from gowns to capes to veils, and since we used our imaginations so much, they were always the most beautiful gowns, the prettiest capes and sheerest veils.

It was the towels that gave birth to *The Legend of the Strange Ladies.*

One day, my two best friends, Chris and Chrissie, and I dressed up in the towels. We each wrapped one around our head. I wore mine draped over my head and across my mouth and nose, with only my eyes showing. Chris's towel was worn over her head like a veil, hanging down to her chin, and Chrissie wore hers draped like a cowl. She held it together with one hand, leaving only a long, narrow slit from forehead to chin.

We were in the shack, giggling at how silly we looked when Chris said, "I know! Let's go out and scare people!"

We quietly sneaked out the back door and hurried around behind the cottage. First, we dashed across the yard to Chrissie's cottage and crept up to the window. We peeked in at Betty, Chrissie's mom. Betty had a wild imagination and an equally crazy sense of humor. She jumped up from her chair and pretended to be scared when she saw us at the window. Then she hurried across the yard to our cottage, stuck her head in the door, and asked if anyone there had seen some strange ladies on the beach.

Mom and Dad played along. They said no they hadn't seen any strange ladies around, but they would be sure to keep their eyes open.

Later, when we came in for a snack, Mom asked if we had noticed some strange ladies on the beach. We said no we hadn't and went back outside. We laughed ourselves silly about her response. We were really convinced that we had fooled everybody.

Several times a week after that, someone would mention seeing strange ladies somewhere on the beach, but no one could ever find them when they went looking. The ladies simply vanished.

Chapter 11 - Rainy-day Amusements

Strange Ladies

This game went on for one whole summer. Unfortunately, by the next summer, we were too old to dress up as strange ladies, and they quietly disappeared into the lore of summertime.

We still laugh about the strange ladies appearance, as if out of nowhere, followed by their mysterious disappearance.

Ah! The fun we had — in the summertime!

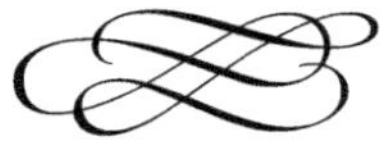

In the Summertime

Chapter 12
Polliwogs and Lucky Stones

There were times when we actually got bored with swimming and we had to look for other forms of entertainment. One of the things we could spend hours at was hunting for frogs and polliwogs. We had a creek that ran from the farm fields to the west, under the road to the beach and out into the lake.

The creek was sometimes clear and running freely and other times thick, green and sluggish. It all depended on rainfall and where the farmers were in their planting season.

The frogs didn't care what the water looked like and neither did we. We caught as many frogs as we could find. We picked up polliwogs by the handfuls, then turned them back into the creek to be caught again on another day — and they were.

Another way that we entertained ourselves was hunting for "lucky stones." Lucky stones were not actually stones. A lucky stone was a small bone, about the size of an adult's thumbnail, found behind the eyes of a fish called a sheepshead. They were considered junk fish and were caught by the fisheries operation of the of the Wisconsin Department of Natural Resources and sold for animal feed.

When the sheepshead die naturally and decompose, the bones behind the eyes get washed up on shore like other small pebbles. We seldom found them just lying on the beach. We had to move the beach stones around to find them. The lucky stones were flat and white, somewhat nondescript. We often found what we thought were lucky stones, only to have them turn out to be pieces of clam shells.

Not everyone was good at finding lucky stones, but I was. I would walk along the shore, just above the high-water line and very gently brush the top layer of stones aside with my foot, looking for the creamy white thumbnail-shape that indicated I had found my treasure. When I saw something promising, I picked it up and looked at the top side.

A true lucky stone would have very fine, shallow grooves on its slightly convex top side. The grooves were caused by the ligament connecting the eye muscles to the top of the head. These grooves formed either an *L* or a *J*. The *Ls* were called *lucky*, and the *J's* were called *jinx*. Later, the meaning of the *J* was changed to Josh, Jeff, or Jennifer, after my son, cousin or niece, depending on who was with me. We collected them all, no matter what we called them. I don't know why, but we usually found more *Ls* than *Js*.

I figured out early on that the best strategy was to walk a stretch of beach one way, always looking, then turn around and go back over the same area. I often found them on the return trip. I guess it was just looking for them from a different angle that made them easier to spot.

I would amble from beach to beach, looking for an optimal hunting shore. It was hard to find them on a sandy stretch because the sand could cover them completely. The beaches with small gravel-like pebbles were best because you could just brush the stones aside and find the lucky stones nestled in amongst the others. The shore in front of our cottage was ideal and the source of the greater part of my collection.

There were sometimes five or six of us hunting for them. Rather often, the others would get tired of looking and go off to do other things, but I usually stayed and hunted for a while longer. Many times I returned to the cottage with my pockets crammed full. At other times, I found few or none, but it didn't matter. I always had a good time, strolling along with the wind in my hair and the gulls crying overhead

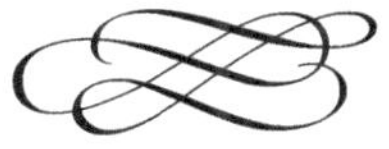

Chapter 13
Suppertime

One of my favorite memories is of the potluck dinners. Looking back at those events, I am still in awe of how spontaneous they were. They just seemed to just happen, usually on a Saturday.

We kids would be entertaining ourselves in whatever fashion we could find, when one of us would notice that several picnic tables had been moved together in one of the centrally located front yards. "Oh good, we're getting together for supper!" somebody would exclaim.

The potlucks started as a way to use up food that was left when it came time to close the cottages for the winter. The piers would have been taken down, the shutters would be on the windows, and the electricity would be ready to turn off.

Then someone would go out and set their picnic table for dinner. Then a neighbor would carry their table over and set it up next to the first one. Before long, everyone got into the act. Someone would bring a grill, if they had something to cook on it. We'd all bring our dishes and silverware and have a party.

We either ate what was provided by the group or, if there were leftovers, they were taken home by whoever decided that they didn't want to cook the next day.

Over the years, we gathered more and more often. Once our friend, Jim, brought 12 dozen ears of sweet corn to roast. We were all sure that there would be plenty of corn left over for another meal for everyone, including the Laughtons, who had seven children. We were wrong. We ate like magicians — we made all the corn vanish in a heartbeat!

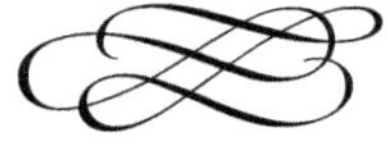

In the Summertime

Chapter 14
Fishing Frenzy

When I was nine or ten, my older sister, Beth, was asked to watch us. Mom and Dad had gone out for part of the afternoon and evening.

That day a couple of us were on our pier when someone saw fish schooling. We all ran, grabbed our rods and our night crawlers, and started fishing.

We always had a supply of nightcrawlers around for those of us who had a sudden, irresistible urge to fish off of a pier. We saved the coffee grounds that Mom and Aunt Emmy Lou generated every day and sprinkled them on the ground under the cottages. That caused the nightcrawlers to come to the surface, where we could pick them up and put them in a bucket of dirt that we kept in the shrubbery behind our cottage.

We each dashed onto a different dock. We could see the fish darting around just under our feet, flitting back and forth. They roiled the water everywhere we looked, and we were roiled with excitement.

One or more of us fished off the pier every day. Sometimes we caught a perch or a white bass, but we seldom caught more than one or two. And now there were hundreds of fish frothing up the water at our very feet.

On this particular day, we caught white bass. As fast as we could bait our hooks and drop them in the water, they bit. When we ran out of worms, we used corn (easy to grab and stick on a hook). Then we used whatever we could find, including, but not limited to, marshmallows. Finally we ran out of bait, so we dropped the empty hooks in the water. The fish just kept on biting.

We hooked a fish, unhooked it, and threw it into a bucket filled with lake water. When our buckets were full, we dashed in to shore, dumped them in the nearest fish tank, and ran out to catch more. I think we probably caught 50 to 100 fish that afternoon, both large and small.

Beth, as the oldest and the one in charge, had the task of cleaning and filleting them for us. My brother should have been there to help her, but as usual, he had disappeared at just the moment he was needed.

When mom and dad got back that evening, the freezer was filled with at least a couple of hundred 3-to-6-inch fish fillets. Beth vowed she would *never* do that again, no matter what kind of fish were schooling!

In the Summertime

Chapter 15
Storm's Coming!

Of the many dramatic storms over the years, there are a few that stand out in my memory. I'm not sure that the storms were really that much worse than others I've witnessed on the lake. It's just that I was very young and the windows in the cottage were very large.

The severity of a storm would be amplified or diminished, depending on the direction from which it approached. If it came from the west, look out! It would be stronger because it was coming across the lake, and there was nothing to slow it down.

When the storms began after bedtime, we left the shack and hightailed it for the cottage. If the storm was from the north, we sometimes sat in the screened porch and watched from there. Otherwise, we all found a good place in the living room to watch the light show.

One storm that I will always remember was one that started out innocently enough, but as we watched, turned into a once-in-a-lifetime spectacle. About midnight we began to notice an increase in the intensity and duration of the lightning. We were sitting in the cottage, watching the storm through the picture windows. The flashes of lightning and the claps of thunder were both fascinating and frightening. Within an hour, the storm had strengthened to such an extent that the night sky was constantly light with just short flashes of darkness. The booming and rumbling of the thunder went on without interruption. I haven't seen lightning that intense or heard the booming and crashing that constant since the night of that unforgettable storm.

The second storm that left an indelible impression was a daytime storm. The seven of us were already in the cottage because our parents knew the storm was coming.

Whenever storms were predicted, we hustled out to gather up all the lawn chairs and anything else that might blow around and cause damage. It's amazing how much damage a lightweight lawn chair can do in a wind storm.

The storm increased in strength, and my cousin, Betty, decided to get some pictures of the lake in the storm. She was walking between our cottage and her family's cottage when there was a sudden gust of wind and an ear-splitting sound. *Crack!!*

We looked out of the side window just in time to see Betty drop to the ground. A large branch from the cottonwood tree had broken off (the *crack* we had heard), glanced off the right side of her head, and then smacked her on the shoulder. She ended up with a scratch on her face and a very, very sore shoulder.

It was a good lesson for all of us young 'uns. *Don't wander around outside during a storm!*

There were several other storms that were fascinating, but none as dangerous as these two.

However, there was a third storm that was almost as exciting, but very short lived. We had all been tucked into bed in the shack. No one of us was asleep yet. Sleep never came quickly with seven of us whispering and giggling in one big room.

We all sat bolt upright at a sudden, terrifying crash. We dashed onto the screened porch just in time to see a wall of sparks flying past the cottage from the direction of the lake. It was an indescribable sight! I remember thinking, just for an instant, that we were watching the end of the world. Then all at once, we started laughing when we realized that the crash was not from thunder or lightning, but from the hot grill blowing over and sending a shower of sparks to the wind. It was not the end of the world after all. Just the embers from the grill blowing in the gale.

I can still close my eyes and see the sparks flying past the cottage. It makes me shiver, all these years later.

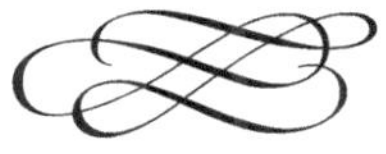

Chapter 16
I've Got Him!

My mother and father used to throw parties at the lake for the sales reps who worked for Dad's company. One time we were cleaning and preparing food, activities that entailed quite a bit of going in and out to set up tables and chairs on the front lawn.

I was in the kitchen with Mom when we heard Beth yell. We dashed out of the kitchen to see what was wrong. Just as we stepped into the living room, we saw something skitter around the corner into the bathroom, with Beth hot on its tail. And it definitely did have a tail. Dad came in from outside to see what the commotion was all about.

He stepped through the front door just in time to see Beth dashing into the front bedroom with a broom in her hand. She was yelling, "Close the door. I've got him!"

Dad called out, "Got who?"

I yelled, "Chipmunk!" and slammed the bedroom door.

We stood in the living room listening to the banging and cussing going on in the bedroom. Beth could sometimes be picturesquely vocal. Mom turned one way, Dad turned the other, and they each dashed out a door. Mom ran back in with a an old wooden box. Dad ran back in with a shotgun. Dad got there just ahead of Mom. He opened the door just far enough to squeeze through it and slammed it behind him. Dad mumbled something and we heard Beth shriek. The door opened, Dad grabbed the box from Mom, set it on the bed, and quickly stepped out, closing the door behind him.

There was more thumping and cussing. Finally, we heard Beth shout, "Uh, I've got him, but…"

We cracked the door open carefully. There was Beth, standing on top of the dresser, holding the box against the ceiling. We stood laughing uncontrollably at the picture before us, afraid that Beth might fall, but at the same time picturing what would happen if the chipmunk escaped.

Dad went out, returned with a piece of cardboard, and got up beside Beth. She lowered the corner of the box and Dad gradually slid the cardboard across the top. They climbed down from their precarious perch

Chipmunk

and carried the box up to the field behind the house, where they released the terrified chipmunk.

When they returned, Mom and I asked about the gun and the muffled conversation.

Beth said that when Dad rushed in with the shotgun, she had said emphatically, "You can't shoot him. Not in here!"

Dad had replied, "For Pete's sake. I'm not going to shoot him. I'm just going to whack him when you shoo him out from under the bed!"

I think Beth's solution was the better one.

We all went back to our preparations. The story of capturing the wild animal that had invaded the cottage was the hit of the party.

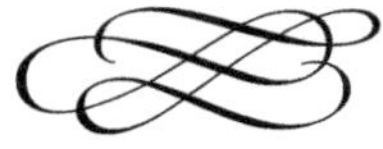

Chapter 17
The Outhouse

In my childhood, the cottages had outhouses. Some cottages also had small septic systems, but they weren't large enough to stay ahead of an entire family's daily use. So except at night, we all used the outhouses. They were disinfected, so none of them smelled like an outhouse. As a result, we didn't mind using them. Ours had one seat, so it only took up half of the space inside. The rest was used for storage. We kept the water skis, the fishing poles, buckets, paint and paint supplies, boxes, broken tools, and a myriad of other things in it.

We referred to ours as "the W. O. W." — the Wonderful Outhouse Woodshed.

It seemed like someone was always knocking on the door, needing this or that. We were always arguing about someone's needing whatever it was at that immediate moment. "Why do you need it while I'm in here?" we'd complain. The response was usually, "You stay in there way too long. I need the skis [or the fishing poles, the bait bucket, or whatever]."

Dad always got up early and went out to the W.O.W with his newspaper. He'd sit there with the door open and enjoy the silence at the beginning of the day. Sometimes a chipmunk would come and sit just outside the door and share the silence with him.

Once, when my cousin, John, and I were young, we accidentally locked Jim Laughton in his outhouse. It had a hook on the outside of the door, as well as inside. They didn't have a latch on the door, so there was a hook-and-eye on the outside to prevent the door from blowing open when no one was around.

John and I were walking home one afternoon. We saw that the Laughton's outhouse door was unlocked and decided that it should really be locked. We had no idea that anyone was inside.

I'm sure the adults were relieved when a new septic system was put in out there. But I think all of the young ones rather missed the outhouses.

When I was young, we would occasionally meet some of the other lake people at our cottage for Thanksgiving dinner. We used the fireplace and the kerosene store for warmth. Our family would usually come out the day before to get the cottage ready.

We never knew what we would encounter when we turned down the lane. On one occasion, we drove into the lane and realized that the snowbanks were so high that we couldn't even see the cottage. We looked for the big cottonwood tree that grew beside the outhouse. Using that as our guide, we lugged everything up and over the snowbank.

While we unloaded the car and started schlepping stuff over the snowbank, Dad fired up the kerosene stove.

There was no running water during the winter months, so we spent quite a bit of time dashing out to the spigot beside the cottage. It connected to an artesian well that flowed year round.

You're probably wondering why I'm including this anecdote in a chapter entitled "The Outhouse." Well, even in the middle of winter, we had to use the out-house. It was not only cold walking to the outhouse, it was cold inside, and there was always a cold up-draft. Believe me, no one sat in there with a book or paper in the middle of a cold November day in Wisconsin! And no one interrupted you to retrieve their water skis.

One Thanksgiving I shrugged into my heavy outdoor coat and headed to the W.O.W. When I turned to close the lid, I brushed the edge of my jacket, and the pencil case in my jacket pocket plummeted into the hole.

I was frantic. The brand-new fountain pen that Dad had bought me for school was in that pencil case. I just *knew* he would be mad! When I returned to the house and told him what had happened, he said, "Don't worry. We'll go to Gruener's and get new supplies when we get home."

I was stunned. I wondered why he wasn't mad. I found out later that he and others in the family had lost things down that hole before, so he couldn't very well be mad at *me*.

The cold outhouse was the only drawback to those November holiday sojourns.

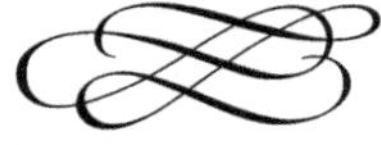

Chapter 18
Ouch!

One day, Kris and I were swimming. None of the neighbors were at the lake, so we were by ourselves. We were out at the third sandbar. We counted sandbars starting at the end of the pier. Kris had convinced Mom to watch us, so there was no problem with our being out so far in the lake.

We had worked our way out to the sandbar and were goofing around doing handstands, somersaults, and twirling until we got dizzy, when Kris yelled. I had just come up from a handstand when I heard her. By the time I had gotten the water out of my eyes, she was headed towards shore. I had no idea why she was going in, but I was out too far to be left alone. I started to follow her in. It was quite deep between the sandbars. I couldn't walk all the way in, so I started to bounce up and down as I walked and swam towards the shore. By the time I got to the pier, Kris was nowhere in sight.

I was tired and a bit scared, because I had no idea what had happened.

I had been under water, so I didn't heard her telling me why she was heading in. It turned out that she had stepped on something sharp. The cut on her toe was bad, but not serious, and Mom said I had done exactly the right thing by bouncing my way along, rather than trying to swim all the way in. I was so young enough that I wasn't a strong swimmer yet. I felt good that Mom had noticed what I did while dealing with Kris's toe.

When Kris reached the pier, Mom asked her why she had left me out in the lake by myself. She replied, " I cut my toe on something. Someone should go out and get Martha. She might drown. I didn't want to leave her, but my toe really hurt.

Mom reassured Kris that it was all right, that everything had turned out ok.

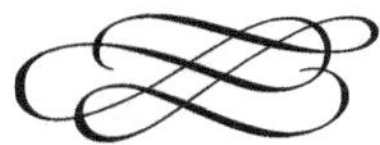

Chapter 19
Boats, Boats, Boats

Motor boats, fishing boats, sailboats, sailboards, canoes, and dinghies. The families on our beach had them all.

Those who liked to fish would put all their gear in their boat and head out to their favorite spots. They would spend most of the day out on the lake, depending on how the fish were biting.

We all had "speedboats," generally with 35-50 horsepower motors. Everybody also had at least one sailboat or sailboard, and some families had one or more of each.

One of the real treats of living at the lake was when the whole family would pile into the boat and head for the harbor. It was only a mile or so from the cottage, but Dad always took the long way. We'd set off in the direction of the harbor, then turn and go in a different direction for a while. Eventually, Dad would head back towards our original destination.

When we got to the harbor, Dad would pull up beside the gas pumps. We kids would all jump out and head for the store for ice cream cones. When he finished filling up, Dad would come in, get himself a cone, and pay for the cones and the gas. Then we'd all jump into the boat, turn around, and head for home. When I was young, I would crawl into the bow of the boat and sit on the extra seat cushions for the ride home.

We had a canoe that was not used daily, but several times a month, Mom and Dad would put it in the water and go for a paddle after supper. We young 'uns would do the dishes and clean up the kitchen while they went for a canoe ride in the cool, quiet evenings when the sun was setting and the lake was as smooth as a mirror.

My personal favorite was the dinghy. It was about five feet long and easy for a small girl to handle. It was painted white with red gunnels. After I had grown up and moved away, I thought about that dinghy, and realized that the gunnels had been painted with the same red paint as the cottage. One way to show where it lived, I guess!

Dad would get up early to drive into town for work, but before he left, he would take a minute to put the dinghy in the water and tie it to the pier.

I loved seeing that little boat tied there. I just knew it was waiting for me to untie it, put the oars in the oarlocks, and row out onto the lake. I would stay out on the water, fishing and paddling around for as long as I was allowed. Eventually though, someone would call me back to shore. Those quiet times out on the lake in that little boat were just about the only times that I was truly alone.

Chapter 20
Rex

We had an adorable dog named Rex. He was half German shepherd and half basset hound. (I can see the wheels turning in your head, and you're right — he was goofy looking.) There were very few people Rex didn't like. You will meet two of the ones he didn't like here.

It's *My* Chair!

Rex didn't like Don. Don was a nice man, but he didn't know how to interact with dogs. He came from a "cat family." His wife was my cousin, Betty, and they had the cottage just to the south of us.

Everyone at the lake had many different kinds of lawn furniture: chairs, tables, hammocks, and lounge chairs. At our cottage, Rex "owned" one of the lounges, but he would get off if we politely asked him to.

One afternoon, some of us were sitting on the front lawn, enjoying a quiet, clear lazy day. The silence was broken only by the twitter of birds and the occasional splash of a fish jumping. Dad and Rex were each sleeping in a lounge chair. The rest of us were in various chairs and the hammock.

Don wandered over to join the conversation and spend some time with us.   Instead of bringing a chair with him, he stopped by Rex's lounge chair and ordered, "Out! I'm sitting here." Rex stood up, turned around, and lay back down with his back to Don.

Dad knew that Rex wouldn't get off for Don, so he said, " Rex, *please* get down." Rex did. Then he sat down facing away from Don, who had no idea that he had just been snubbed by a dog.

For the rest of the summer, Rex totally ignored Don. He would either waddle away or turn his back when Don was around.

The next story is another example of Rex's expressing his opinion about someone he didn't care for.

Witch Alice

Roy and Alice Tucker owned the cottage that was the marker for one end of our beach. They came out to the lake and fished all weekend. When they came in off the lake on Sunday, they packed up their fish, closed up their cottage and drove home. If they arrived and the lake was too rough to go fishing, they pretty much stayed indoors.

Roy was a nice man, quiet and friendly when he was by himself. Alice, on the other hand, was not a nice woman. She yelled at us when we walked across her yard. She especially disliked dogs and went out of her way to shoo them away. She would come out of her cottage with a broom if a dog even got close to her yard.

Rex was extremely smart and very sensitive to peoples feelings. One day, Dad went over to help Roy with whatever it was he was doing, and as he usually did, Rex tagged along. Roy patted him, and Rex wagged his tail. Then he began to sniff around. Suddenly, Alice appeared at the front door. Everyone, including Rex, stood breathlessly waiting to see what she would do.

Alice stood in the doorway for a moment, then turned and walked back into the cottage. A moment later she returned with a hambone, which she held out to Rex. He just stood beside Dad, not looking at her or the bone. Dad told Rex that it was okay; he should go and get it. Rex looked at him as if to ask, "Do I have to?" Dad said, "Go." Rex stood up, walked slowly to the steps, reluctantly took the bone, and started towards home.

The moment he crossed out of their yard and into the neighbors', Rex dropped the bone and continued to our house without looking back. Dad was embarrassed. Beth was proud of Rex.

Rex

Alice seldom yelled at us or the dogs after that incident. I don't know if seeing Rex drop the hambone finally woke her up, or if Roy talked to her.

I guess we should have quit calling her Witch Alice at that point, but by that time it had become a habit.

In the Summertime

94

Chapter 21
Slippery Kids

I married and moved to Oklahoma, but summers at Lake Winnebago continued, with my own children sharing the delights of the red cottage. Naturally, with young children in tow, there were "incidents." Once, when two of our three children were small, they got their grandpa into trouble with their grandma and me.

It must have happened on a weekend, because Dad was home during the daytime.

Mom and I were going to town to run some errands and pick up groceries and dry cleaning. As we got ready to leave, Mom asked Dad if he was prepared to watch the two youngsters. "Sure, I've *got* this. We'll be fine," he assured us. Mom and I looked at each other, hesitated a moment, shrugged, and set out for town.

We finished our errands, and after a stop at the bakery to buy freshly-made goodies, we headed back to the lake.

I questioned Mom once or twice about Dad's watching the kids. "I think it will be fine. Your dad is quite good at that sort of thing," she said confidently.

We had been gone three hours by the time we pulled into the driveway, glad to be home. Mom parked the car and we began to unload the laundry and the groceries. We each carried in a load of grocery bags. We said hi to dad as we came in. "Where are the kids?" I asked.

"Oh, they're playing on the back porch. They've been real good. They've been playing quietly the whole time." Uh oh. That could only mean one thing! *Trouble!*

Mom and I gave each other a knowing look and headed to the porch at a run.

We got to the door and stopped dead in our tracks. In spite of the scene before us, we burst out laughing. There were my little daughter and son, sitting on the floor, completely covered in Vaseline! They didn't just have some on their arms and legs — they were covered from head to toe.

Mom called to Dad to come out to the porch. He laid down his paper and walked out to join us. As he stepped through the door, we heard a noise that was a combination snort, cough, and laugh. I asked him how long they had been like this. Dad admitted that he didn't know. They had been playing quietly for a while, so he didn't think it was necessary to check on them.

I explained that that was exactly the time to check on them. Playing quietly for more than a few minutes meant that they were almost certainly doing something they shouldn't be doing. So, while Mom and I tried to gather up two very slippery children covered in a thick, slippery layer of Vaseline, Dad dutifully went out and unloaded the car for us.

Mom and I rolled up our sleeves and began the process of getting those two little urchins out of their incredibly slimy clothes and cleaned up. It took four showers (there was no bathtub) and the entire huge new bottle of dish soap to get them back to some semblance of normalcy. We also used almost an entire bottle of shampoo. Then we spent the rest of the day washing their clothes, by hand, since there was no washer or dryer at the cottage.

Needless to say, we educated Dad on the art of watching young kids.

#1 Check on them often.

#2 Listen for the chatter of small voices.

#3 Most importantly, if there is an extended period of silence, check on them *immediately*! In this case, silence is not golden. It's hurry-up-and-check-on-them time!

We finally got our slippery kids un-slicked, and Dad was much more vigilant in watching the grandchildren after that.

In the Summertime

Epilogue

Aunt Emmy Lou still comes to the lake every summer. She's 101 years old now, the last of the previous generation. She spends her winters in California with her daughter Sue, but in late May, Emmy Lou arrives at the lake, driven there by Sue. She usually stays for several weeks to visit with all who have come for summertime at the lake.

After Sue gets her mother settled in and comfortable, she returns home and the summer routine begins. Several of the "kids" who grew up at the lake have bought cottages and now live there year 'round. They have developed a routine that allows them to keep an eye on Emmy, while still keeping up the traditions we all grew up with.

Emmy gets up each morning and brews a pot of coffee. About nine, anywhere from one to six people arrive at her house with breakfast items and a newspaper. Later in the day, one of them will call her and offer to bring either lunch or supper. A couple of times a week, everyone gets together and takes her to their favorite restaurant, just up the road from the beach.

Emmy Lou has become the still point around which we all spin.

What will we do when she is no longer here?

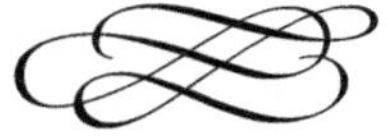

9 781640 079236